How Many Veggies?

by Phil Vischer

Tommy
NELSON™

Thomas Nelson, Inc.

Nashville

Art Direction:
Ron Eddy

3D Illustrators:
Tom Danen, Robert Ellis,
Aaron Hartline, Adam Holmes,
Mike Laubach, Joe McFadden,
Daniel López Muñoz, Joe Sapulich,
Ron Smith and Lena Spoke

Render Management:
Jennifer Combs and Ken Greene

Copyright © 1997
by Big Idea Productions

Illustrations Copyright © 1997
by Big Idea Productions

Published in Nashville, Tennessee, by Tommy Nelson™,
a division of Thomas Nelson, Inc.

Library of Congress Cataloging-in-Publication Data
Vischer, Phil.
    How Many Veggies? / by Phil Vischer.
        p. cm.
    Summary: Bob the Tomato is joined by nine other vegetables until
his boat becomes so full that it begins to sink.
    ISBN 0-8499-1488-4
    [1. Vegetables — Fiction. 2. Boats and boating — Fiction.
3. Counting. 4. Stories in rhyme.] I. Title.
PZ8.3.V74Ho 1997
[E] — dc21
                              97-23986
                                CIP
                                AC

Printed in the United States of America

98 99 00 01 02 03 BVG 9 8 7 6 5

Dear Parent

We believe that children are a gift from God and that helping them learn and grow is nothing less than a divine privilege.

With that in mind, we hope these "Veggiecational" books provide years of rocking chair fun as they teach your kids fundamental concepts about the world God made.

– Phil Vischer

President
Big Idea Productions

Bob the Tomato is taking a trip.
A day on the sea will be fun!
How many veggies are on his small ship?

The answer, of course, is 1!

Larry the Cucumber joins Captain Bob.
Could *he* find a place on the crew?
Maybe first mate — he'd be great for the job!

Now on the boat, there are !

Two little veggies are taking a trip.
Junior says, "What about me?
I've got some crackers and soda to sip!"

Count them again, 1 – 2 – 3 !

Larry says, "Hey! Who will push us along?
I'm not very good with an oar.
Let's call Mr. Nezzer, because he's so strong!"

Now on the boat, there are **4**!

Junior says, "Captain! Our numbers are growing!
Soon we'll be rowing, the wind will be blowing,
But tell me please, how will we know where
    we're going
If no one is sitting up there?
We need someone up in the air!"

The gourd they call Jerry is next to arrive.
His compass and spyglass would help them survive!
So, quickly they vote him shipmate number 5!

And send him up high in the air —
To stare at the sea from his chair.

Five little veggies, no room for another,
The perfect vocational mix!
'Til Jerry says, "Boy, I sure do miss my brother."

And Jimmy becomes number !

"Six is enough!" Bob remarks to his men,
"At least it's not ten or eleven."
But Percy jumps in, and when Bob counts again —

1 – 2 – 3 – 4 – 5 – 6 – 7 !

"Only one thing that we're missing!" says Larry,
"A parrot! Now that would be great!"
Then Laura shows up with her pet parrot, Harry.

And now on the boat there are 8!

Eight little veggies and one silly parrot
(Who came, you'll remember, with Laura the Carrot).
"The weight, sir!" says Junior, "our boat cannot bear it!
We're headed for trouble, I think —
Our boat is beginning to sink!"

Yes, eight little veggies, all trying to bail!
Starting to argue and whine —
"I'm coming!" yells Archie, "and I've got a pail!"

He jumps in, making it **9**!

Nine little veggies, all wet to their knees,
Beginning to shiver and shake,
Turn to see something come out of the trees
That makes their hearts quiver and quake!

Goliath the giant — a big, bumpy pickle —
Runs down to the dock with a shout!

"I'm no good at sailing, but I just love bailing!
So I'm going to help you guys out!"

L E S

A king cobra is covered in scales. The scales are dry and not slimy. Most snakes' scales have a pattern.

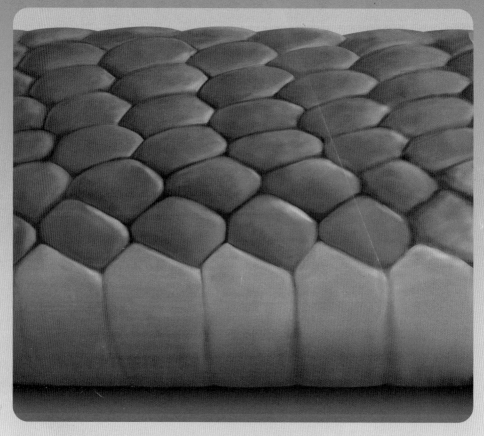

The skin of a king cobra looks like this. The belly scales are the widest.

INTERESTING FACT
A group of cobras is called a quiver.

KOMODO DRAGON SKULL

This is the skull of a Komodo dragon. It looks a bit flat, like the skulls of crocodiles and alligators.

SHARP FACT

Anything that tries to escape it gets cut by the sharp side of its teeth.

WARNING!

You do NOT want to get bitten by a Komodo dragon.

OTHER KOMODO DRAGON NAMES

A Komodo dragon is also called an ora or a land crocodile.

KING COBRA SKULL

This is the skull of a king cobra. It does not have much of a skull. Its brain is mostly unprotected.

FUN FACT
The study of snakes is called ophiology or serpentology.

King cobras do not chew their food. In addition to fangs, they have small upper and lower teeth to pull food into their mouths. They swallow their prey whole.

QUESTION
Would you like to become a scientist and study snakes?

KOMODO DRAGON'S FAVORITE FOOD

Komodo dragons love to eat small mammals. They also eat lizards and snakes. They kill by tearing their prey to shreds.

GROSS FACT
Komodo dragons can easily eat half of their body weight.

DID YOU KNOW?
A Komodo dragon's venom prevents blood clotting. Its victims sometimes bleed to death.

DISGUSTING FACT
If a Komodo dragon eats too much hair, bones, nails, and scales, it coughs up a giant pellet.

KING COBRA'S FAVORITE FOOD

Snakes are the favorite food of king cobras. Their scientific name means "snake-eater."

JUST ATE

ONE MONTH

TWO MONTHS

FUN FACT
After eating a large meal, a king cobra might not eat again for one or two months.

WITH LEGS

Look at the skeletons of the Komodo dragon and king cobra. What differences do you notice right away?

VALUABLE FACT
The government of Indonesia minted a gold coin in honor of the Komodo dragon.

The Komodo dragon has legs and toes. It also has a distinct tail.

WITHOUT LEGS

The king cobra has no legs, fingers, or toes. It has many ribs, making its body look like one long tail.

NEWLY

Mother Komodo dragons lay about twenty-five eggs per clutch. Komodo dragon babies live in trees. They eat bugs, small lizards, rodents, and eggs.

DEFINITION
A clutch is a group of eggs laid by birds or reptiles.

GROSS FACT
Young Komodo dragons roll in animal waste to protect themselves.

BORN

Here is a king cobra baby. A king cobra is the only snake that makes a nest. It looks like a bird's nest.

KING COBRA TRIVIA

After making a nest, mother king cobras lay between twenty and fifty eggs at a time.

STRANGE BEHAVIOR

A Komodo dragon sometimes eats its own children. Young Komodos are smart enough to escape up a tree.

MORE STRANGE BEHAVIOR

A king cobra can spread its rib bones and make itself appear larger. This behavior is called making a hood.

HOOD!

NO HOOD!

FUN FACT

The design on the back of this king cobra's head are called spectacle markings.

ZOO

You can see a Komodo dragon in some zoos. The experience can be disappointing, because reptiles spend many hours never moving.

QUESTION

Would you like to become a herpetologist?

26

PETS

If you travel to India or Thailand, you might see a street performer doing tricks with a cobra.

FUN FACT
Some people have king cobras and other snakes for pets.

The Komodo dragon walks around looking for food. If hungry, he would eat almost any animal. He doesn't notice the king cobra under nearby grass.

INTERESTING FACT

Of all the animals on Earth, the Komodo dragon probably most resembles the look and walk of a dinosaur.

The cobra has no interest in the Komodo dragon. Snakes like to eat things they can swallow whole. The Komodo dragon is way too big!

The Komodo dragon wanders a bit too close. It raises its head, spreads its hood, and makes a growling sound. It is a warning to back off!

The cobra just wants to be left alone. The Komodo dragon circles around some more.

YIKES!
Not only can the king cobra slither on the ground, it can also swim and climb trees.

The clumsy Komodo dragon steps off the cobra's eggs by accident. The cobra strikes fast, biting the leg of the intruder! As soon as the cobra's fangs sink into the Komodo dragon's leg, they unload their venom.

The Komodo dragon walks a few steps, then starts to breathe heavily. Its legs get wobbly. It can't see, gets dizzy, and falls over.

The king cobra has killed the Komodo dragon with one deadly bite! Maybe next time, the Komodo dragon will bite first.

WHO WOULD WIN?®

TARANTULA VS. SCORPION

What would happen if a tarantula met a scorpion?
What if they were both in a bad mood and had a fight?
Who do you think would win?

SCIENTIFIC NAME OF TARANTULA: "Theraphosa blondi"

Meet the tarantula. There are almost 900 species of tarantulas. In this book, we will feature the largest, the goliath birdeater tarantula.

FACT
Most tarantulas are the size of your hand.

DEFINITION
An arachnid is a class of arthropods that live on land. Spiders, mites, and ticks are arachnids.

WOW
A fully grown goliath birdeater tarantula is 12 inches across.

Tarantulas are hairy spiders. Spiders have four pairs of legs. Spiders are in a group of invertebrates called arachnids.

SCIENTIFIC NAME OF
SCORPION:
"Leiurus quinquestriatus"

Meet the scorpion. There are more than 1,500 known species of scorpion. We will use the death stalker scorpion in our battle.

CAREFUL!

You do NOT want to get stung by a scorpion.

FACT
The largest scorpion is the emperor scorpion, which is 8 inches long. The death stalker scorpion is 3 inches long.

Scorpions are also arachnids. They have two claws and an extended tail. The scorpion has a stinger on the end of its tail. Next to the stinger is the telson, which is filled with poison.

TARANTULA'S BURROW

Many tarantulas live in burrows. They usually dig their own tunnel and then leave a web at the entrance to stop intruders and water from coming in. Sometimes a tarantula will move into an abandoned burrow of a snake or mouse.

Tarantula's territory

DEFINITION

A burrow is a hole or tunnel in the ground dug by an animal for a place to live.

SCORPION'S BURROW

Scorpions live under rocks, under branches, and just about anywhere they can safely hide. Most scorpions hide during the day and come out at night.

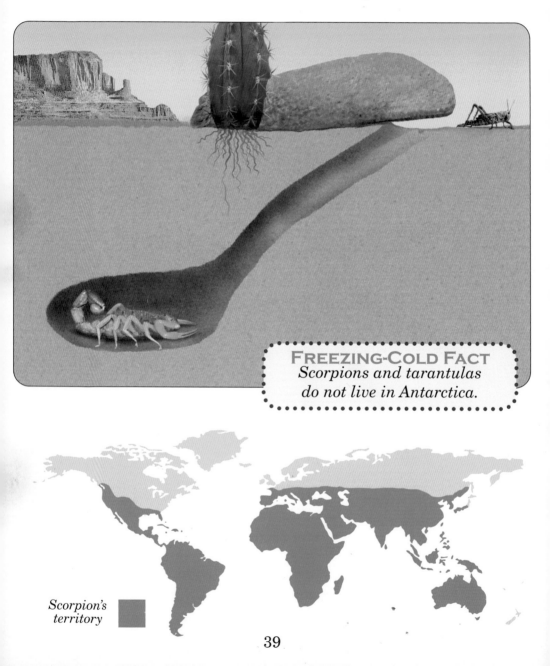

FREEZING-COLD FACT
*Scorpions and tarantulas
do not live in Antarctica.*

*Scorpion's
territory*

TARANTULA ANATOMY

Notice the segmented body, which is divided into two parts. The legs come out of the front part, the thorax. The back part is the abdomen.

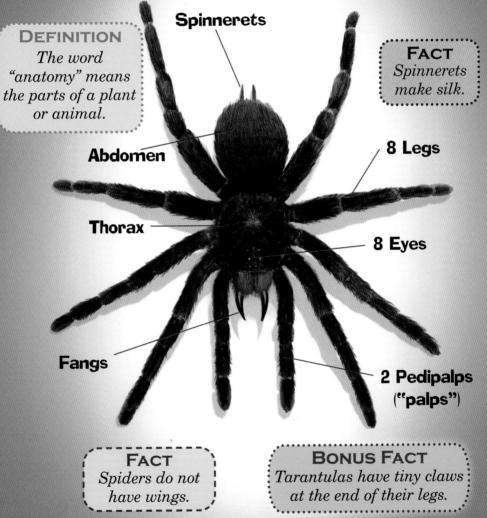

Spinnerets

DEFINITION
The word "anatomy" means the parts of a plant or animal.

FACT
Spinnerets make silk.

Abdomen

8 Legs

Thorax

8 Eyes

Fangs

2 Pedipalps ("palps")

FACT
Spiders do not have wings.

BONUS FACT
Tarantulas have tiny claws at the end of their legs.

It looks like tarantulas have ten legs, but they don't. The two legs beside their mouths are called palps. They are like arms. They help the tarantula move their food around.

SCORPION ANATOMY

Scorpions have two eyes on the top of their thorax and three to five pairs of eyes on the sides. The side eyes are called lateral eyes.

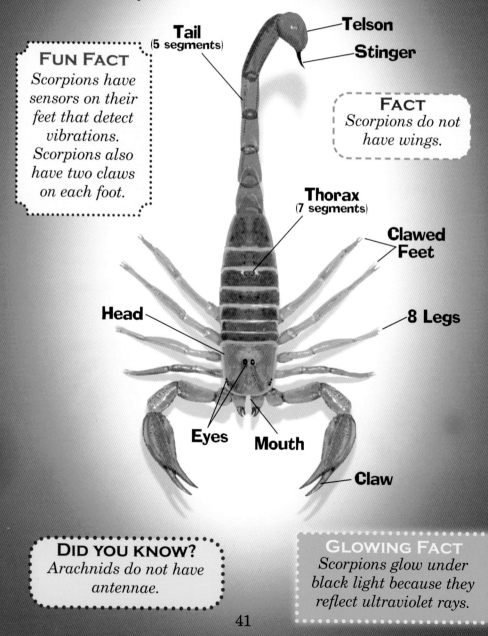

Tail
(5 segments)

Telson

Stinger

FUN FACT
Scorpions have sensors on their feet that detect vibrations. Scorpions also have two claws on each foot.

FACT
Scorpions do not have wings.

Thorax
(7 segments)

Clawed Feet

Head

8 Legs

Eyes

Mouth

Claw

DID YOU KNOW?
Arachnids do not have antennae.

GLOWING FACT
Scorpions glow under black light because they reflect ultraviolet rays.

TARANTULA WEAPONS

The tarantula's mouth has quite a bite. It carries poison in its fangs.

BOTTOM VIEW

FANGS

MOUTH

FACT
All tarantulas are predators.

YIKES! DISGUSTING!
Tarantulas throw up digestive juices onto their prey.

Tarantulas rub their legs against their hairy bodies and shoot hair at their attackers. This is called urticating. It is a nasty weapon that makes some animals cough and have trouble breathing.

SCORPION WEAPONS

Two claws that can bite.

FACT
Scorpions are different colors depending on where they live.

A stinger that can pierce. Its poison can paralyze a scorpion's victims.

YIKES!
Scorpions also throw up on their prey.

The scorpion has two little pincers in its mouth.

TARANTULA COUSINS?

Some animals are similar to a tarantula. Many other creatures in the animal kingdom also have eight legs.

TARANTULA

CRAB

DID YOU KNOW?
The name "tarantula" comes from an Italian dance, the tarantella.

TICK

MITE

ALL IN THE FAMILY

You could say that a scorpion is a "land lobster."

FACT
Shrimp have ten legs.

SCORPION

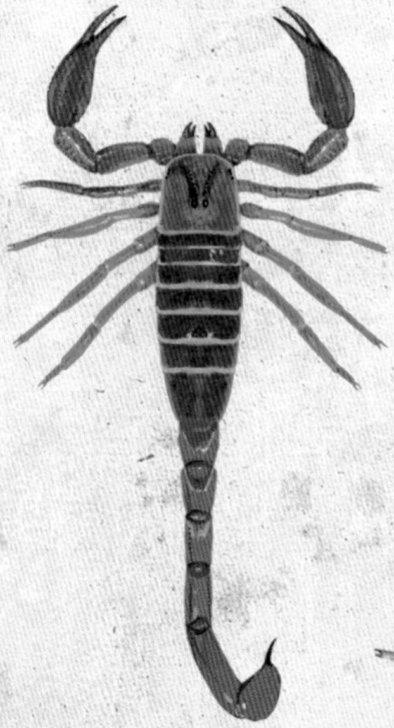

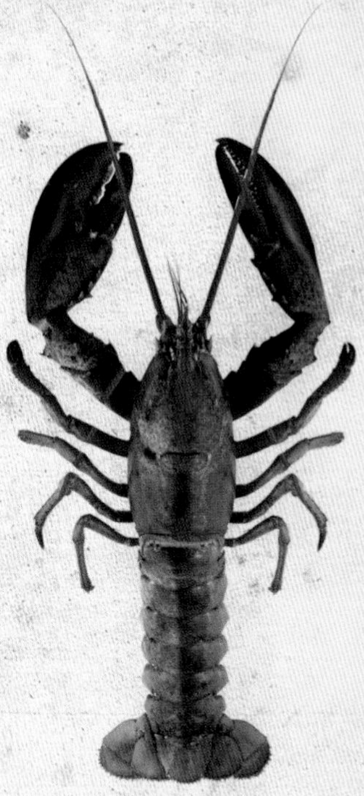

LOBSTER

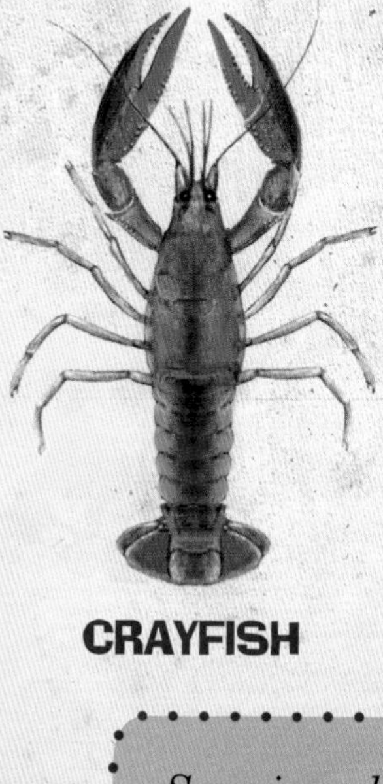

CRAYFISH

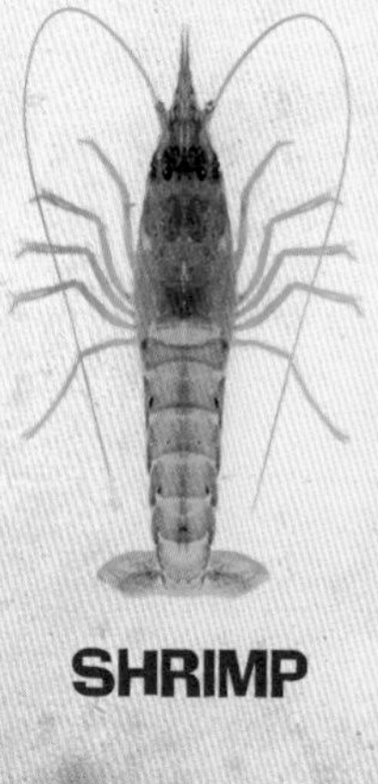

SHRIMP

FACT
Scorpions, lobsters, and crayfish all have eight legs. Scientists think they are related.

YUMMY

Tarantulas are not vegetarians. They are carnivores. Tarantulas hunt and eat insects, other arachnids, tiny mice, lizards, snakes, and small birds.

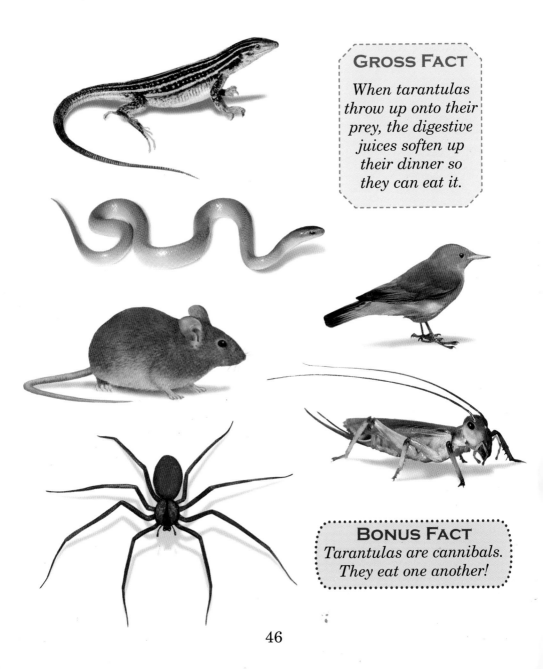

DELICIOUS

Scorpions are not hunters. They wait for food to come to them. Scorpions mostly eat insects, spiders, and other bugs.

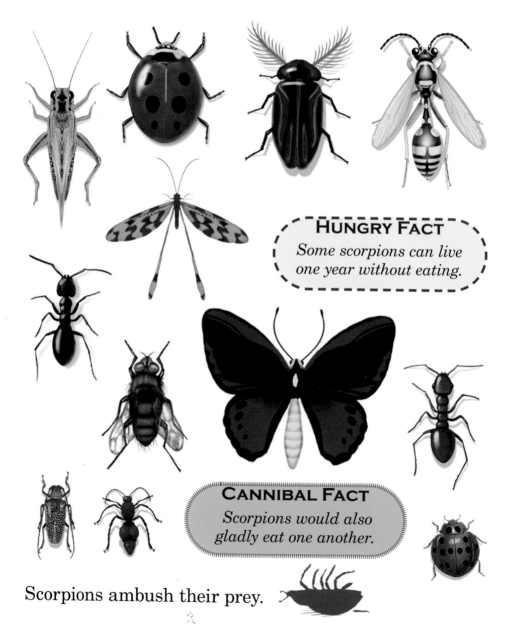

HUNGRY FACT
Some scorpions can live one year without eating.

CANNIBAL FACT
Scorpions would also gladly eat one another.

Scorpions ambush their prey.

MOLTING

Humans and other mammals have bones inside their bodies. Tarantulas and other arachnids have their skeletons on the outside of their bodies.

FACT
Tarantulas have an exoskeleton. An exoskeleton is an exterior shell.

To grow larger, the tarantula sheds its exoskeleton. This is called molting.

FACT
Mammals have an endoskeleton.

DID YOU KNOW?
When tarantulas molt, they shed their entire skin, including the linings of their mouth, respiratory organs, and stomach.

WE MOLT, TOO

Scorpions also have an exoskeleton. You could say that scorpions climb right out of their own skins.

This is not a picture of two scorpions. On the left is the scorpion's old shell. On the right is the same scorpion with its new exoskeleton.

QUESTION
How can you tell which is the shell?

ANSWER
The one without eyes!

49

TASTY!

Some people eat tarantulas. They roast them over a fire on a stick and eat them like you would eat a marshmallow. Tarantulas are said to be delicious.

This is a bowl of roasted tarantulas. People in Asia, Africa, and South America enjoy eating them.

QUESTION
Do you think your school cafeteria should serve tarantulas for lunch?

DID YOU KNOW?
People from the Amazon rain forest squish the guts out of the abdomen and cook it like scrambled eggs.

BETTER THAN A HOT DOG?

Humans also eat scorpions. And not just a few people. Millions of people eat scorpions!

Which would you prefer? Scorpions on noodles? Or scorpions on rice and beans? Maybe for dessert you can lick a scorpion lollipop.

FACT
People in China eat millions of tons of scorpions per year.

51

DREAM THIS

This is a tarantula in attack mode. If you were ant-sized, this is what it would look like if you were fighting a tarantula.

THE TARANTULAS

The Tarantulas would be a great name for a football team.

IMAGINE THAT

The scorpion has a three-pronged attack—left claw, right claw, and a piercing tail. Pretend you are fighting a giant scorpion. It would look like this!

BIG ANCIENT FACT
A fossil of an eight-foot-long sea scorpion was recently discovered.

THE SCORPIONS

The Scorpions would be a cool name for a baseball team.

YOUNG TARANTULAS

A mother tarantula does not take care of her young. As soon as the spiderlings are born, they are on their own.

DID YOU KNOW?
Female tarantulas can live for more than twenty years.

WOULD YOU BELIEVE?
A baby spider is called a spiderling.

SCORPION BABIES

Scorpions are good mothers. They carry their cute little babies on their backs.

THINGS TARANTULAS FIND DIFFICULT

Finding glasses with eight lenses.

Finding matching shoes.

Finding a hairdresser who won't run away.

PLACES YOU DON'T WANT TO FIND A SCORPION

On your face while you've been sleeping.

Near the bathroom.

In your lunch box.

The tarantula is climbing a tree. The tips of its legs are like little needles. It has no trouble climbing.

The scorpion, as usual, is hidden under a rock. It doesn't want to bother anyone. It is waiting for some food to walk by.

Soon it is dusk. The scorpion takes a peek outside.

The scorpion gets a surprise. The tarantula jumps on top of it. Normally the tarantula would use its legs and palps to pin down an insect and jab it with its mouth fangs. But the scorpion fights back. The tarantula does not like the snapping scorpion claws.

The scorpion scrambles and escapes.

The scorpion uses its claws and tail to fight. It backs off, then runs right at the tarantula. It grabs the tarantula's palps with its claws, then jabs one of its legs. The scorpion shoots venom into the tarantula's leg.

The tarantula is bigger than the scorpion, but now one of its legs is numb. The tarantula flips the scorpion over, but the scorpion gets right back up and jabs another leg.

While the tarantula wonders what's wrong with its legs, the scorpion jabs it in the body.

The poison starts working, and the tarantula eventually stops moving. The scorpion will eat the tarantula.

WHALE
VS.
GIANT SQUID

What would happen if a whale swam near a giant squid? They are both carnivores, or meat eaters. What if they had a fight? Who do you think would win?

SCIENTIFIC NAME OF SPERM WHALE:
"Physeter macrocephalus"

Meet the sperm whale.

> **BIG FACT**
> *The blue whale is the largest animal on Earth.*

> **COLORFUL FACT**
> *Whales have red blood.*

> **RUNNER-UP FACT**
> *The sperm whale can grow to be 60 feet long and weigh 50 tons.*

It is one of the world's largest whales. All of the biggest whales are baleen whales, which means they have no teeth. The sperm whale is unusual. It is a big whale that has teeth, but only on its bottom jaw.

This whale looks like a big head with a tail. Its scientific name means "blower with a big head." It is the largest of all toothed whales. The sperm whale has the largest head of any animal that has ever lived on Earth.

DID YOU KNOW?

The sperm whale has a blowhole at the front of its head.

LONG FACT
Its head can be 20 feet long.

SCIENTIFIC NAME OF
GIANT SQUID:
"Architeuthis dux"

Meet the giant squid.

> **FACT**
> *Squid, octopuses, nautiluses,
> and cuttlefish are cephalopods.*

> **BONUS FACT**
> *On restaurant menus, squid
> is often listed by its Italian
> name, "calamari."*

A giant squid is a mollusk. A squid belongs to a group of mollusks called cephalopods. *Cephalopod* means "head foot." A squid looks like a head attached to legs. It has eight legs and two extra feeder arms. The legs have suction cups. The feeder arms have hooks and suction cups on the ends that act like hands.

The giant squid has fins for steering. It propels itself by sucking water into its head and squeezing the water out. A squid works the same way as a jet engine.

GIANT FACT
The largest squid are the giant squid and the colossal squid.

DID YOU KNOW?
A giant squid brain is the size and shape of a small donut.

A giant squid can be 60 feet long and weigh 450 pounds. Most giant squid that have washed up on beaches are 20 to 30 feet long. That's a lot of calamari!

MAMMALS

Whales are mammals. The people reading this book are mammals, too. Here are some other mammals:

Dolphin

Monkey

SMART FACT
The sperm whale has the largest brain of any animal that has ever lived.

Kangaroo

Dog

Rat

DEFINITION
A mammal is a hairy or furry warm-blooded animal that has a backbone and feeds milk to its young.

MOLLUSKS

Squid are mollusks. Here are examples of other mollusks:

Mussel

DID YOU KNOW?
"Mollusk" and "mollusc" are both correct spellings.

Octopus

Clam

Snail

DEFINITION
A mollusk is a soft-bodied animal that usually lives in water and has a protective shell.

Cuttlefish

EYES

The eye of a sperm whale is only about 2 inches wide.

FUN FACT
A sperm whale can dive down half a mile. There is hardly any light at that depth.

EYES

Here is a human eyeball.

Here is a giant squid eyeball in comparison. The giant squid eyeball is the largest eyeball in the world. It is as big as a basketball. Its giant eyeballs allow the squid to see at great depths.

TEETH

The sperm whale has long teeth. The teeth are shaped like sidewalk chalk. Notice that it has no teeth on its upper jaw. When a sperm whale closes its mouth, its bottom teeth fit into the indentations in its upper jaw.

FUN FACT
A sperm whales has 20 to 25 teeth on each side of its lower jaw.

BONUS FACT
You can tell how old a sperm whale is by the layers in its teeth.

DID YOU KNOW?
Whalers used to carve beautiful designs on whale teeth and whale bone. This type of art is called scrimshaw.

BEAK

Between its eight legs and its two feeder arms is the squid's mouth. It does not have teeth. Squid have a beak. It looks like a parrot's beak.

FACT
The tip of a squid's beak is hard and tough, but the lower end is more rubbery.

The beak is made of chitin, a material which is like your fingernails.

TAILS

The tail of a sperm whale can be 16 feet across. Whales have horizontal tails.

TRY THIS
Use a measuring tape to mark 16 feet across your classroom. Wow! That is a wide fluke!

Other fluke shapes:

blue whale

humpback whale

sei whale

right whale

FINS

The body of a giant squid is called the mantle or torso. At one end are fins. The giant squid can use its fins to steer. It can also reverse the motion of its fins to swim backward.

FACT
People have seen giant squid jump completely out of the water.

FUN FACT
Squid have three hearts.

BONUS FACT
The squid can also steer itself with its legs.

OIL

Sad but true: Before the discovery of petroleum, whales were a source of oil. It is estimated that 600,000 sperm whales were killed for their oil.

FACT
There are 6 to 8 barrels of oil in the head of a sperm whale.

BONUS FACT
The first time a whale was killed for oil was in 1690. The busiest whaling years were in the 1700s and 1800s.

This is what a typical Nantucket whaling ship looked like. They would often leave port and return four years later.

If whalers harpooned a whale and the whale took off, it was called a Nantucket sleighride.

CASH REWARD

No one has ever caught a giant squid and kept it alive. If you ever catch one, it may be worth $1,000,000. Someone will be willing to pay it.

ONE MILLION DOLLARS

$1,000,000
AWARD

DINNER

Sperm whales eat giant squid, squid, stingrays, octopuses, and fish.

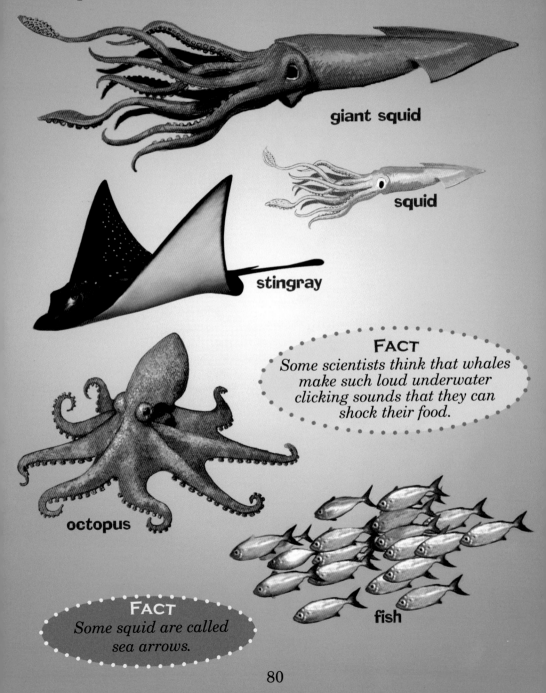

giant squid

squid

stingray

FACT
Some scientists think that whales make such loud underwater clicking sounds that they can shock their food.

octopus

fish

FACT
Some squid are called sea arrows.

SUPPER

Giant squid eat fish, shrimp, and other squid. They grab food with their long feeder arms. The feeder arms have sharp spines on the ends. They pull the food into their beaks.

FACT
Squid arms and legs are also called tentacles.

close-up of a feeder arm

COLORFUL FACT
Giant squid have blue blood.

SPEED

A sperm whale can swim 25 miles per hour.

DID YOU KNOW?
A *Dall's porpoise* can swim faster than 50 miles per hour.

FUN FACT
The fastest fish is the sailfish. It can swim 90 miles per hour.

DEPTH

A sperm whale can dive half a mile deep.

1/2
MILE

AMAZING FACT
Sperm whales can hold their breath for up to 2 hours. They usually submerge for about 45 minutes.

sperm
whale

*Empire
State
Building*

ocean floor

SPEED

A giant squid can swim 20 miles per hour.

ocean floor

underwater canyon

It is not known how far a giant squid can dive.
It can dive deeper than a whale. A giant squid is
more agile than a whale. It can change direction
suddenly and can swim backward.

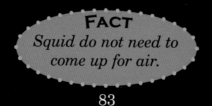

FACT
Squid do not need to come up for air.

ECHOLOCATION

In deep water, the whale relies on echolocation to find its way around. It finds its food by bouncing sound signals off its prey. The whale is lucky compared to a squid. A giant squid cannot hear.

DEFINITION
Bouncing sound back from its prey is called echolocation. The whale uses this to learn where its food is.

SOUND FACT
Sonar is the location of objects through sound waves. Bats, whales, shrews, and some birds have sonar. Submarines have sonar, too!

There are many things we don't know about the sperm whale. We don't know why they do not have teeth in their top jaw. We do not know how many get killed by giant squid.

INK

We don't know how long a giant squid lives. Some scientists think it is only three years.

SECRET WEAPON
Squid blow black ink at their attackers. This is called billowing.

DINNER FACT
Some famous chefs use squid ink to make black pasta. It is called squid-ink pasta.

We don't know how deep they can dive. We don't know how many there are. We don't know where they live, but it appears they prefer deep, colder water. We don't know why no one has been able to catch one alive.

DID YOU KNOW?
There are no known freshwater squid.

FAMOUS WHALE

Moby-Dick is a famous American novel written by Herman Melville. The whale in the story is a giant albino sperm whale. Moby Dick bit the leg off a captain, who vowed revenge. At the end, the whale rams and sinks the ship.

FUN FACT
Moby-Dick *also became a famous movie.*

The story was based on a real sperm whale that rammed and sank the Nantucket whale ship *Essex*. A nonfiction book was written about the event, called *In the Heart of the Sea* by Nathaniel Philbrick.

FAMOUS LEGEND

For hundreds of years, sailors around the world have been afraid of giant squid. A legend is that they come out of the deep and are so large they can swallow a ship.

SCHOLASTIC CLASSICS

20,000 Leagues Under the Sea

...Verne

With an introduction by Bruce Coville

SCHOLASTIC

Science fiction writer Jules Verne wrote about a giant squid attacking a submarine in a novel called *20,000 Leagues Under the Sea.*

The whale dives. It is looking for food. It sends out sound waves, hoping to find a tasty meal. It senses a few small fish. The whale is hungry. It is looking for a nice giant calamari dinner.

A giant squid is in deep water and out of range.

The giant squid decides to move to shallower water, an easier place to find food. Most fish and squid live in water less than 200 feet deep.

The whale senses the giant squid a quarter of a mile deep. It dives deeper.

The giant squid doesn't notice the whale right away. The whale clicks a few sounds, locates the giant squid, then attacks with its mouth open. The whale grabs a small piece of one of the squid's arms.

The giant squid blows ink in the whale's face, then darts away.

The whale swims after the giant squid. The squid sees the whale and decides to attack first. The squid realizes it is in for a fight. It puts all its legs and feeder arms on the whale. Suction cups and hooks scrape the whale's skin.

The squid tries to hold the whale down until the whale runs out of air. Its plan doesn't work.

The whale maneuvers and bites a chunk of the squid and a few of the squid's arms. A few more bites and the giant squid is in deep trouble.

The whale thinks the giant squid is delicious.

The whale wins, but he has sucker and scratch marks all over his head. That fight hurt!

HYENA VS.
HONEY BADGER

What would happen if a hyena and a honey badger met each other? What if they had a fight? Who do you think would win?

HYENAS

There are four types of hyenas.

The spotted hyena is the largest and strongest hyena.

spotted hyena

This is the rarest species of hyena. It is found mostly in the Kalahari Desert in Africa.

brown hyena

This is the smallest hyena.

striped hyena

An aardwolf is also considered a hyena but it eats mainly insects.

aardwolf

Hyenas are mostly nocturnal, which means they hunt and move about at night.

BADGERS

There are several types of badgers. Badgers are short, stocky mammals with strong jaws and thick, tough skin.

This badger is also called the Eurasian badger.

FACT
Honey badgers are also mammals.

Eurasian badger

This badger prefers to live on prairies. It eats small mammals such as squirrels.

MASCOT FACT
The University of Wisconsin–Madison's sports teams are named the Badgers!

North American badger

About half of the honey badger's diet is snakes, including venomous snakes.

DEFINITION
Venomous means using poison to kill their prey.

honey badger

How would you describe a honey badger? Fearless and ferocious!

MEET THE SPOTTED HYENA

In this book we will feature a spotted hyena. Its scientific name is *Crocuta crocuta*.

IT'S OKAY TO LAUGH

The spotted hyena is also known by many as a laughing hyena.

98

MEET THE HONEY BADGER

The honey badger's scientific name is *Mellivora capensis*.

FACT
*Honey badgers are omnivores.
That means they eat everything,
including animals and plants.*

Honey badgers have dark fur around their bodies with white fur on their heads and backs. They look like they might be made of chocolate with vanilla frosting on top.

DON'T BE CONFUSED

African wild dogs are not hyenas but sometimes look like them.

African wild dog

hyena

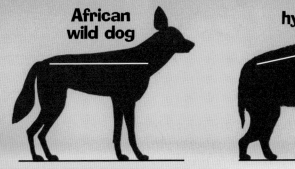

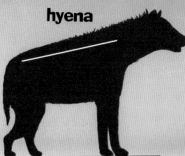

FACT
The legs of an African wild dog are all the same height.

FACT
A hyena's front legs are longer than its back legs. Hyenas have a long, thick neck.

RELATED

Badgers are related to otters, polecats, wolverines, and weasels.

otter

> **JUST THINK**
> *The honey badger is also related to the sea otter.*

polecat

> **DID YOU KNOW?**
> *A honey badger rarely drinks water. It gets fluid from the blood of snakes and other creatures it eats.*

wolverine

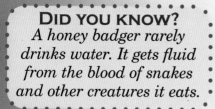

> **FACT**
> *Honey badgers also eat melons to get more fluids.*

weasel

PACK

A group of hyenas is called a cackle. Hyenas are often found in large packs.

Other **COLLECTIVE**, or **GROUP**, words:

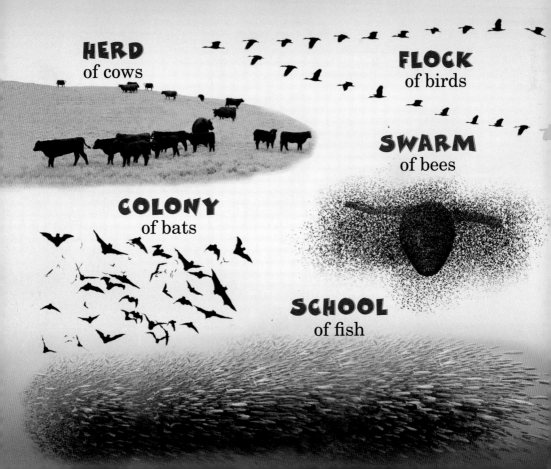

HERD
of cows

FLOCK
of birds

SWARM
of bees

COLONY
of bats

SCHOOL
of fish

ALONE

A group of honey badgers is called a cete. However, most honey badgers prefer to travel and hunt alone.

More **COLLECTIVE** words:

PARLIAMENT
of owls

MURDER
of crows

PRIDE
of lions

CRASH
of rhinos

AFRICA

Hyenas live in Africa and Asia. Most live at the edges of forests and on savannas.

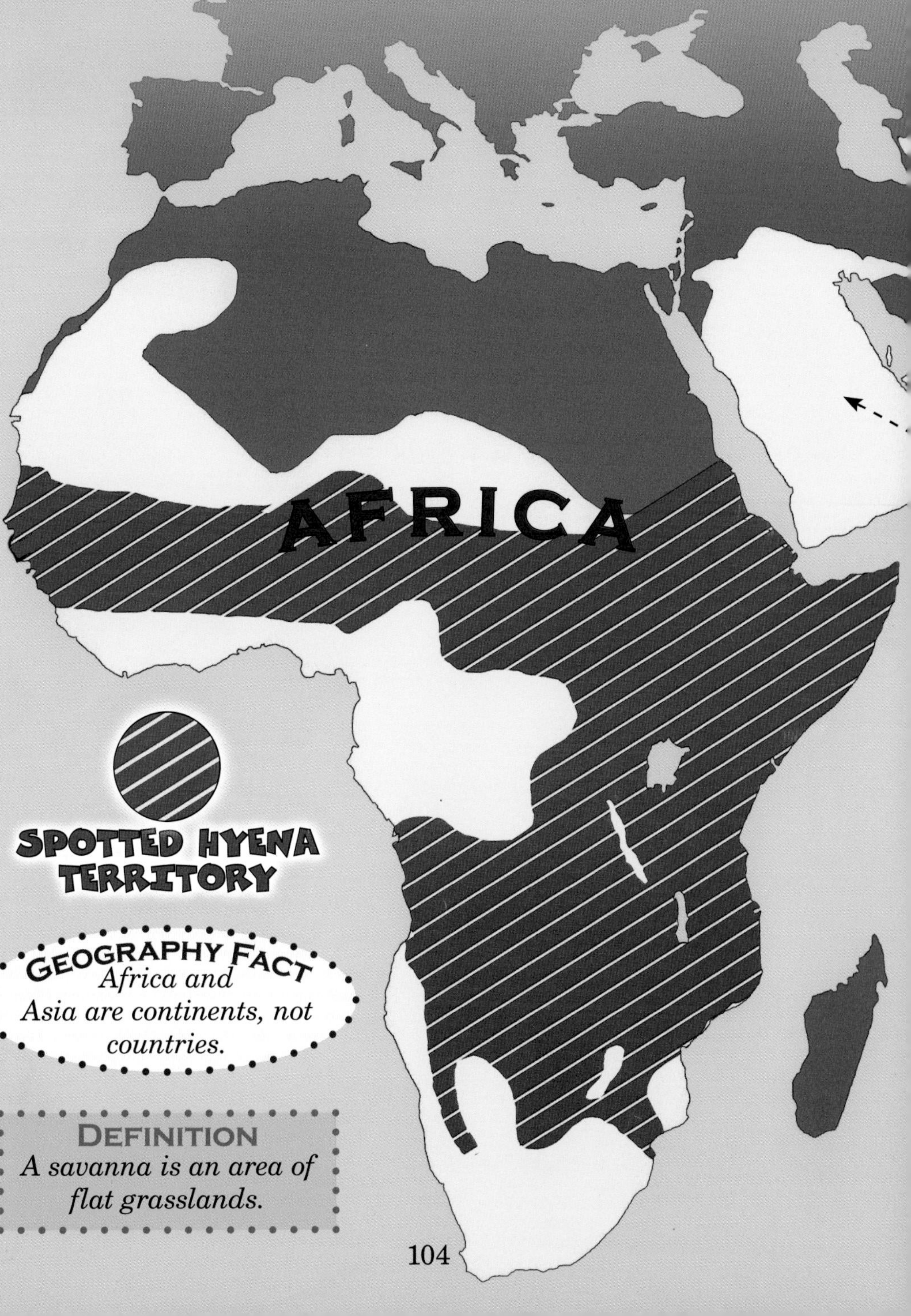

AFRICA

SPOTTED HYENA TERRITORY

GEOGRAPHY FACT
Africa and Asia are continents, not countries.

DEFINITION
A savanna is an area of flat grasslands.

104

ARABIA AND INDIA

The honey badger lives in Africa, on the Arabian Peninsula, and much of India.

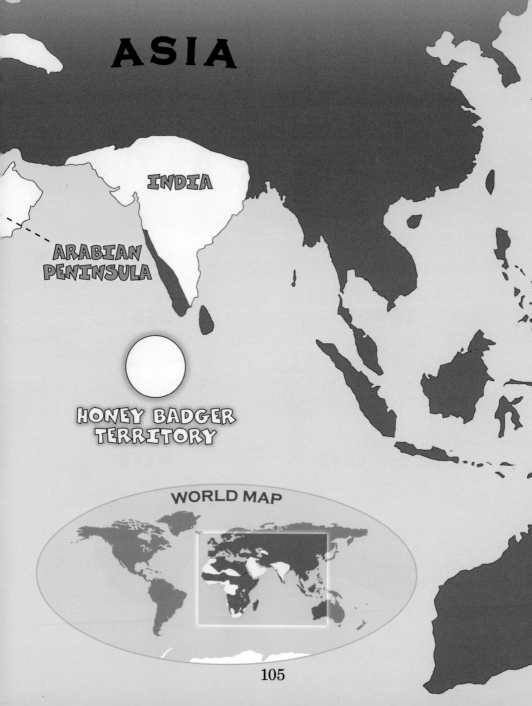

ASIA

INDIA

ARABIAN PENINSULA

HONEY BADGER TERRITORY

WORLD MAP

DEN

Hyenas live in underground rooms, chambers, and tunnels called a den.

Other animals have different names for their **HOMES**.

Beavers live in a **LODGE**.

Birds live in a **NEST**.

Polar bears live in a **SNOW CAVE**.

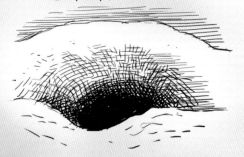

Bees live in a **HIVE**.

Can you think of more names of the places animals live?

*The publisher would like to thank the following for their
kind permission to use their photographs in this book:*

Photos ©: 16: Skulls Unlimited International, Inc.; 17: Skulls Unlimited International, Inc.; 18: Jonathan &
Angela Scott; 22: Michael Pitts/Nature Picture Library; 23 top: Sandesh Kadur/Nature Picture Library; 27:
Hans Neleman/Getty Images; 48: Tom McHugh/Science Sources; 49: Andres Morya Hinojosa/DanitaDelimont.
com; 50: Radius Images/Alamy Images; 51: Ronaldo Schemidt/Getty Images; 55 bottom: McClatchy-Tribune
via Getty Images; 55 top: David M. Dennis/Animals Animals-Earth Scenes; 74 bottom right: Dirk Renckhoff/
Alamy Images; 78 center: akg-images; 78 bottom: Mary Evans Picture Library Ltd/agefotostock; 81 bottom right:
Louise Murray/Science Source; 86: Look and Learn/Bridgeman Images; 102 top: Anup Shah/Minden Pictures/
Superstock, Inc.; 106: Aberson/Getty Images; 141 coin: United States Mint. All other photos © Shutterstock.com.

Thank you to Dr. Stephen Durant, rugby player supreme!
Dedicated to Pat Perry, Pat Barr, Mary Perdew, and Deanna Hill.
This book is for Connie Ross, a New Hampshire reading legend.
Thank you to Joyce Hinman and Marvia Boettcher.
To my favorite falcon, Rose Wandelmaier.

—JP

Thank you to Mr. Winslow Homer.
Thank you to John Singer Sargent.
This book is dedicated to Edward Hopper.
For our little honey badger, Clara Elizabeth Breslin.
To the favorite falcon's loving family.

—RB

ISBN 978-1-338-84155-8

10 9 8 7 6 5 4 3 2 1   22 23 24 25 26

Printed in China 38
This edition first printing, 2022

Book design by Kay Petronio

-TABLE of CONTENTS-

Who Would Win?
Komodo Dragon vs. King Cobra 4

Who Would Win?
Tarantula vs. Scorpion 34

Who Would Win?
Whale vs. Giant Squid 64

Who Would Win?
Hyena vs. Honey Badger 94

Who Would Win?
Falcon vs. Hawk 124

Who Has the Advantage? 154

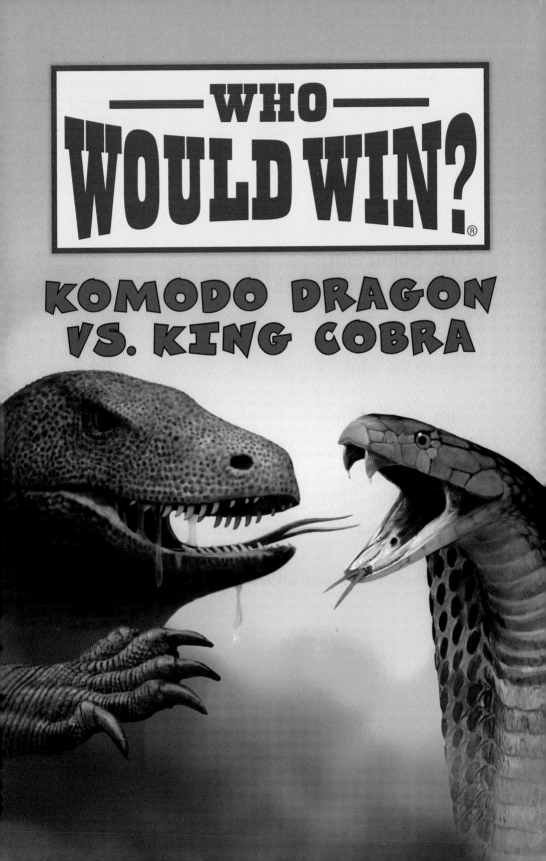

WHO WOULD WIN?®

KOMODO DRAGON VS. KING COBRA

What would happen if a tough Komodo dragon came face-to-face with a deadly king cobra? What if they were both hungry? If they had a fight, who do you think would win?

SCIENTIFIC NAME OF
KOMODO DRAGON:
"Varanus komodoensis"

Meet the Komodo dragon. The Komodo dragon is the largest lizard in the world. It grows up to ten feet long and can weigh three hundred pounds.

DEFINITION
A reptile is a cold-blooded animal covered in scales. Turtles, snakes, lizards, crocodiles, and alligators are reptiles.

FACT
Komodo dragons live on four Indonesian islands: Komodo, Rinca, Flores, and Gili Motang.

SCIENTIFIC NAME OF
KING COBRA:
"Ophiophagus hannah"

Meet the king cobra. A king cobra can grow up to eighteen feet long. The king cobra is a venomous snake that can weigh up to twenty pounds.

DEFINITION
Venomous means poisonous.

DEFINITION
A snake is a reptile that has no arms, legs, movable eyelids, or external ears.

FACT
King cobras live in India, China, Southeast Asia, Indonesia, and the Philippines.

TEETH

Komodo dragons have teeth. Their teeth are unusual for a land animal. They are serrated, like a shark's teeth.

DANGEROUS FACT
Serrated means jagged, like a saw.

FANGS

King cobras have fangs. A fang is a long hollow tooth used to inject venom.

DID YOU KNOW?
If a king cobra's food is too large, it can unhinge its jaws and widen its mouth.

DEADLY

There are only three known poisonous lizards: the Gila monster, the Mexican beaded lizard, and the Komodo dragon. In addition to venom, the Komodo dragon has dangerous bacteria in its mouth.

> **DEFINITION**
> *A lizard is a reptile with two pairs of legs and a tail.*

GILA MONSTER

MEXICAN BEADED LIZARD

VENOM

A king cobra bite is deadly. A king cobra does not have the deadliest poison of all snakes. But it injects the most poison. Its poison is a neurotoxin. One king cobra bite has the strength to kill an elephant—or twenty people.

DANGEROUS DEFINITION
A neurotoxin is a poison that paralyzes its victim's nerves and muscles.

SNAKE TRIVIA
Some species of cobras can spit their venom, but a king cobra cannot.

FORKED

The Komodo dragon has a forked tongue. It splits into two
sides. A Komodo tongue is sensitive. When it flicks out its
tongue, it can detect where a deer might be nearby.

TONGUES

The king cobra also has a forked tongue. It smells with its tongue. Its tongue can also sense motion and temperature.

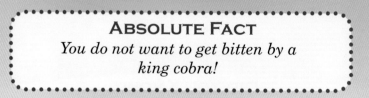

ABSOLUTE FACT

You do not want to get bitten by a king cobra!

S C A

The skin of a Komodo dragon looks like this.

BONUS FACT
Reptiles have scales.

DID YOU KNOW?
Butterflies, moths, and most fish also have scales.

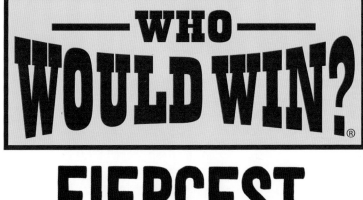

FIERCEST
FEUDS